I S

ANNE SIMPSON

IS

(POEMS)

McClelland & Stewart

Library and Archives Canada Cataloguing in Publication

Simpson, Anne, 1956–
Is / Anne Simpson.

Poems.
ISBN 978-0-7710-8051-7

I. Title.

PS8587.I5453318 2011 C811.'6 C2010-905408-3

Library of Congress Control Number: 2010940064

We acknowledge the financial support of the Government of Canada through the Book Publishing Industry Development Program and that of the Government of Ontario through the Ontario Media Development Corporation's Ontario Book Initiative. We further acknowledge the support of the Canada Council for the Arts and the Ontario Arts Council for our publishing program.

Typeset in Centaur by M&S, Toronto
Printed and bound in Canada

This book was produced using ancient-forest friendly paper.

McClelland & Stewart Ltd.
75 Sherbourne Street
Toronto, Ontario
M5A 2P9
www.mcclelland.com

1 2 3 4 5   15 14 13 12 11

For my sisters,
Jennifer and Susan

(CONTENTS)

Book of Beginnings

1

Cell Division

13

Divide, Break

16

A Cell, a City

17

At the Bottom of the World, a Tree of Gold

21

Counting Backwards

29

The Hives

30

Child

31

Above

32

Is

33

Flood

34

Flood, Translated

35

Flood, Interior View

36

Viva Voce

37

River

46

November

48

Later

49

Life Magazine

50

Aslant

56

Button

57

Dream

58

Boat of Dawn, Boat of Dusk

59

Tonja's Letter

73

Easter

74

In the Night Cathedral, a Tree

75

Clear

76

Double Helix

79

Notes

93

Acknowledgements

94

IS

before you were a cell, dividing into cells and more cells—

before blue before blue deepening and unwinding inside blue before bluegrey before the envelope of morning before opening the crisp envelope of morning before afternoon and afternoon's picked threads before evening before the scattering of evening's fish scales before crumpled dark before tarnished dark before glovesoft dark before world not yet world all undone and unmade thick and ancient furred by weather not yet weather creased and lined rock and water linen-thin water and rock unseamed bulky dense and smooth not birth not death both icy and steamy sounds not yet sounds darkness before darkness and light before light beginning and ending ending and beginning woven and braided and woodsmoke fragrant and not woodsmoke fragrant shot through with glistening and murmuring unmurmuring cloud of murmuring also glistening linen-thin water and rock rock and water unseamed furred by the weather not furred lined creased steamy and icy smooth not birth not death all undone done made and unmade

Now.

You are the world dividing.

You are day divided from night, night from day, minute from minute, hour from hour. Time begins, sliced into now, and then, and meanwhile, and later, so a story can be made of it. Your story will have other stories inside it, but one story, the familiar story, will separate itself and become a plot, full of rising action and falling action, and other stories will become indistinguishable subplots, so that telling them apart will be the same as separating water from water, or separating water from air, or air from water, or separating the waters of the firmament from the waters below.

You are dark inside dark, and within this dark, intricate contraptions of darker darkness. Nightbeing, nonbeing. Things have their places—your place is behind them. But your wish is to soften them, call them back to what they were, what they could have been. This is what you try to say as light begins, grows, diminishes you.

Day, with its extravagances. You take command, expose dust in the corners. But there's something to one side that needles. A time before this. Before the smear on the mirror. Before tinkering. Before the ululation of a siren. Before scarlet. Before latches. Before eyes. Before opening and closing. Before the pecking of this, this, this.

You are spaciousness.
You reach and keep reaching, without meeting resistance.
This is what it is to be above all things.
To be wide and unsullied, yet also to gather.
Gather and let go. The work of the wind in its passing.
No need to possess anything.
In the spaciousness there are many cupboards—empty, empty.
Clouds glide over earth, loosely, and without purpose.
You are clarity and distance. Without clutter.
Without pockets, made for nickels, crumbs, paper clips, or strips of paper from fortune cookies, or words on strips of paper, or paper, or making, or scissoring, or question, or answer, or wind sifting the answer when the question has been forgotten.
Only spaciousness.

You are depth and more depth, earthing and earthed. And silence—about to burst. Here, the grass, new blades. Grass and grass and grass, shoving forward, clover nodding through. Muscling into the world: grass, ferns, sedges, a loose scatter of coltsfoot. On the branches of the tree, hundreds of small red pagodas forming themselves into leaves. Above, the spoon tip of goldfinches, a yellow wing daubed with black, and swallows, pulling at the edges of air. When they die, you'll bring them back into yourself. Cover them, remember them. But this isn't the time; this is the time of damp soil, its metallic scent, and buds about to unsleeve themselves. Smell. Taste. This is where they begin, where they rise. Through you, everything becomes known to itself.

Fire. You are what you embrace—heat, in its thousand costumes. So you consume, thriving on beginnings. A tirade, then a benediction of embers, blackened remnants. Ash, a layer of velvet, dressed up as beauty when it's merely wreckage.

Endlessly spending, losing, spending more. All that is born in you is fluid, slipped and slipped and slipped from one thing to the next. Sliding over and under whatever is firm and solid, when nothing is firm or solid. You have the power of undoing, unmaking. Glint and murmur and rinse, and the cool beginning of silver. Water, a sound at the threshold of hearing, turned inside out. A lover seeking a way in, a way through. Sleek and glimmering as rain, and not rain, but brook and river and lake and ocean, unceasing and open. An answer, withdrawn and reinvented into another answer, rolling and cresting and slapping sand. Pulled back. Never slow enough to hold, to be held. The beating at the rim of the world.

You are making yourself.

Beginning, ending, beginning.

a woman untucking a cotton shirt a man undoing a belt it begins
with a touch just a fingertip along a wrist a zipper unzipped clothes
tossed on a chair and skin against sheets her body opening his
body fine hairs on her arm and soft clefts in his skin puckers and
creases of skin and skin of a wrist thin skin knuckle skin raw silk
skin of an earlobe the skin under his knee warm skin of her stomach
the skin across his back the length of his spine unlocking the black
sky the bone under his cheek whorl of her ear a staircase inside a
nautilus shell his mouth on her mouth his tongue inside her mouth
her tongue inside his mouth his fingers tightening on the flesh of
her thigh her arm around him his arm under her back her legs his
legs bridges her body gliding under his body the tide going out
sand fringed with seaweed bracelets of kelp she's clutching what
slips away and she can't he can't her hands tight on the muscles
of his arms his hands on her hips as they slide into ocean the
sound of his rushing hand in her hair salt taste of his skin back
and forth seal-wet slickness of her body with his body a man a
woman making and unmaking slanted light a woman untucking a
cotton shirt and a man undoing a belt it begins with a touch—

FIGURE I

a woman untucking a cotton shirt a man undoing a belt it begins with a touch just a fingertip along a wrist a zipper unzipped clothes tossed on a chair and skin against sheets her body opening his body fine hairs on her arm and soft clefts in his skin puckers and creases of skin and skin of a wrist thin skin knuckle skin raw silk skin of an earlobe the skin under his knee warm skin of her stomach the skin across his back the length of his spine unlocking the black sky the bone under his cheek whorl of her ear a staircase inside a nautilus shell his mouth on her mouth his tongue inside her mouth her tongue inside his mouth his fingers tightening on the flesh of her thigh her arm around him his arm under her back her legs his legs bridges her body gliding under his body the tide going out sand fringed with seaweed bracelets of kelp she's clutching what slips away and she can't he can't her hands tight on the muscles of his arms his hands on her hips as they slide into ocean the sound of his rushing hand in her hair salt taste of his skin back and forth seal-wet slickness of her body with his body a man a woman making and unmaking slanted light a woman untucking a cotton shirt and a man undoing a belt it begins with a touch—

FIGURE 2

a woman untucking a cotton shirt a man undoing a belt it begins with a touch just a fingertip along a wrist a zipper unzipped clothes tossed on a chair and skin against sheets her body opening his body fine hairs on her arm and soft clefts in his skin puckers and creases of skin and skin of a wrist thin skin knuckle skin raw silk skin of an earlobe the skin under his knee warm skin of her stomach the skin across his back the length of his spine unlocking the black sky the bone under his cheek whorl of her ear a staircase inside a nautilus shell his mouth on her mouth his tongue inside her mouth her tongue inside his mouth his fingers tightening on the flesh of her thigh her arm around him his arm under her back her legs his legs bridges her body gliding under his body the tide going out sand fringed with seaweed bracelets of kelp she's clutching what slips away and she can't he can't her hands tight on the muscles of his arms his hands on her hips as they slide into ocean the sound of his rushing hand in her hair salt taste of his skin back and forth seal-wet slickness of her body with his body a man a woman making and unmaking slanted light a woman untucking a cotton shirt and a man undoing a belt it begins with a touch—

FIGURE 3

Break into break up break down break out break off break open break away break me up take a break don't step on a crack you'll break your mother's back breaking ground breaking record breaking news break the spell break the bank break the ice break a leg the straw that broke the camel's back lucky break seven years of bad luck if you—

Break into laughter break into song break into tears make it or break it break my heart break your heart break his heart break her heart breaking up is hard break this bread sticks and stones may break—

make a break for it break out in a cold sweat knucklebreaker jawbreaker ballbreaker break and enter break it up boys all hell breaking—

And wind, doing what wind does. Rattling a jar of bones.

In Xuankou, a man sets down his cup. The steaming tea begins to shiver.

Silence.

Aftershocks of noise—a gas main, propane tank.

Men crawl in a tilted world, equipped with life-detection equipment, radar. Will they dream of the eighteen-month-old twins found breathing under the body of their grandfather? Or will they dream of a woman with her arms around a boy made of dirt, embedded in dirt? Seven rescuers in red uniforms brushing at the dirt with small brushes, as if the woman and boy were thousands of years old.

City of departure.

In September, anyone can open the doors of the honeycombed palaces, gaze into the storerooms of clover honey, cherry blossom honey. The chambers are furnished in wax. The queen is old. Outside the gates, drones are dying.

Inside, worker bees are listening to syllables of spun light: concert-goers seated on small chairs, straining to catch each phrase.

A city about to leave itself behind.

But first—

Floating city.

A ship, each of the portholes closed. Frigid weather. Inside, a grand staircase,
a palm court, a smoking room, ice chinking in the glasses, and somewhere not far
away, a band playing "Songe d'Automne."

Afterwards,
one piece of sheet music with blue stains;
several broken deck chairs;
one champagne bottle (vintage 1900), unopened;
one foremast running light;
men's toiletry items, including an ivory-handled shaving brush;
sixty-two perfume vials, scattered;
one slipper (for the left foot), with rhinestone clasp and bow;
rows of unbroken dishes;
a skylight revealing the ocean floor.

City of wishes.

At dawn, a man is looking for something. He searches among the larger piles: old refrigerators, freezers, stoves with gaping mouths. Wooden table legs, chair legs. Doors opening into other doors: doors beneath doors. He can't find what he wants, but he keeps walking because of the chill. Wind brushing his hair. He could be a nurse, moving between camp cots in a hospital.

On the other side of the fence, a doe with a fawn. Observers.

Massage your fingers into her scalp. With the shower curtain half-drawn her hair is nearly transparent; the strands are fine. Her head could be that of your grand-mother, your great-grandmother, your great-great grandmother.

Shampoo her hair, rinse it. Do this with care. At the same time, do it briskly, so she won't get cold.

On her hip, taped bandages. Because of the surgery, her legs are bruised with burgundy islands. Indonesian archipelago.

You could pick her up, gently, a package of wet feathers, but she'd rather do things herself. She wants to be in and out of the bath, tucked into bed.

But after her bath, she'll do her exercises.

Hang up the damp towels, go into the garden.

It's October. The souls of the flowers have risen into the cool air. Phlox, daisies, lilies, roses. The leaves of the hostas are yellow, waxy.

You've come to strip the garden for winter. You have shears in your hands.

But you think of your fingers on her scalp, making circles. The way the two of you were quiet.

When you rinsed her hair, she didn't complain. Silver ran down her neck, down her back—music slipping away from the body, returning to it.

Once, as a child, you paused on the stairs. You could see into her bedroom, where she knelt by her bed, concentrating hard. She was lifting you into the air; she didn't know you were crouched on a step, watching through the smooth uprights of the banister.

Lifting her husband, each of her children, and years later, her grandchildren. None of them knew how they were lifted, set down in a different place.

This has always been her work.

Your work is to strip the garden. Then it will be time to leave.

Outside, the roses are drooping, blackened with frost. The weight of summer carried to the gate of autumn.

Inside, she falls asleep with a book in her hands, the same one she's been reading for years, ever since she was a girl. Halfway through, it unfolds into another story. Not the one she was expecting.

Behind the shed, at the top of the ravine's slope: a heap of stalks, weeds, dead leaves. Gather remnants from the garden, toss the day's work.

What lures you down to the creek? That liquid voice, telling its story between moist banks. Coppery leaves on the surface. You imagine all that lies below: dank palaces under the ground. To move there is to move blindly.

When you return to the house, you bring the scent of the underworld with you.

Wash your hands for a long time at the kitchen sink.

You're not the only one to have made journeys. She was there long before you.

Once, she lost her way. Ask her about that. She'll tilt her head to one side, remembering. Then she'll distract you, talking about babysitting her cousins at the farm.

You don't want to hear about the farm, or the cousins. You want to hear about a tree made of gold at the bottom of the world.

Now she's sleeping. One hand lies on the covers.

This is the most difficult work of all, allowing frost to cover the branches, cold dreaming itself into whiteness. Letting the dark come into it.

You'll return to the tumble and kilter of scattered light. April,
nothing held back.

Beloved.

Crocuses, murmuring secrets to earth. Purple, yellow.
Soundless instruments, daffodils. Tulips, their petals. As if girls
had put their wrists together, fingertips touching.

Count back from one hundred, the doctor said, subtracting by seven, ninety-three, I told him, keep going, he said, checking vitals, not wanting to know about Maplehurst, grade seven, eighty-six, I said, straight rows of desks in the math classroom, Miss Haffajee in her green sari, a Venn diagram flowering from the red dot on her forehead, keep counting, he said, seventy-nine, I told him, rain on the Cobequid Pass, the road a dream of water, seventy-two, slippery, and a steep ditch on one side, sixty-five, good, he said, you can stop there, fifty-eight, the guardrail was about twelve feet long, if that, with a jumble of rocks below, but he'd gone to the next bed, to the man who needed a CT scan, fifty-one, forty-four, both of us strapped to boards on the gurneys, heads against blocks, keeping us immobile while the doctor asked the man his age, and the ceiling slid open to the September evening, sharp taste of stars after rain, thirty-seven, a man needing stitches on the back of his head, thirty, twenty-three, velvet of nothing spreading into the darkness of every direction, going on and on, sixteen, nine, two.

THE HIVES

No one in the halls of the Ursuline convent at Bruno.

A faint smell of gas, and a statue of the Virgin Mary gazing
at the honey-coloured carpet, loosened
from its staples. A cold bathroom,
no one in the dining room or the kitchen. Abandoned hive.

The women have gone.

Outside at the firepit, old kitchen chairs and a sofa:
camaraderie.

Folded umbrellas of the cherry trees. Nearby, white boxes nestle
in a circle. The bellows of the smoker are squeezed gently.
Incense of alfalfa and pine cones,
pungency in the air.

The strong hives are sheltered together in wintering cases. Sleep-scented.

Some of the combs are scraped, empty boxes carried to the flatbed truck.
The weak divided from the strong.

Broken necklace of bees in curled, damp grass.

And the living—thousands—roused. Humming.

Wish without a wishbone. One, two,
buckle my—

Spark and strike, lantern light.
One, two. Three is over the hill and far away.

No last one, round one. Spoonful of moon.
This little piggy, that little wolf. Dimes and nickels
and a penny for your thoughts.

One, two.

Me, you.

Star in the west, blanket of blue.

Don't we need some people? We could use pipe cleaners.

The people are out shopping. Anyway, we don't need them.
God doesn't need them.

God wouldn't be God without people.
People have bodies so they can do what God can't.

What could you do without a body?

Is snow as years, lightly. Is your face back then, your hands.
Is mine and not. Is the low branch, ice moon split by the blade
of the low branch.
Is kiss, cool, kiss. Is snow. Is always
inside never.
Is years. Is the pileated woodpecker, the hammer of a beak.
Is goldsmith. Is time, shimmered.
Is my arms is your arms is my shoulder is your shoulder is my neck is your—
Is not love. Is.
Is the box of feathered white, opened.
Is opened, is closed. Is day and night, feathered.
Is a bird inside your chest, inside mine. Is fear, that hammer.
Is fear of opening. Is courage.
Is the frailty of daylight, falling to pieces around us.
Is music under your eyes, music touched with a finger. Mine.
Is mine is yours. Shadows under your eyes.
Is children, is ducks, is dogs. Is sleep, sleep, sleep.
Is snow. Is glass. Is snow.
Is your eyes back then. Saw, see, saw.
Is you, now. Is snow. Is your hands, lightly, years.
Is your head in your hands. Is the sound of the spoon in the cup.
Is ruby under cloud. Is morning, is fire.
Is held. Is more than.
Is laughter, feathered. Is low branch, high branch.
Is a rosehip, winter's lantern:
one, two, three, four.
Is moon, married to sky. Unmarried. And married.
Is night's cloak, embroidered. Is yours is mine.
Is speechlessness. Is touch. Is snow.

FLOOD

after *Bent Passage* (1981, graphite on wove paper) by Betty Goodwin

A woman pauses above a fold in the land. No longer a stream, the stream that had been there.

Water, moving. Trees, moving.

Objects carried past. From above, beads, undone.

The woman's vertigo as she stands apart, looking down.

At night, she thinks of the rush of water around the ankles of the spruce, oaks, sugar maples.

Sky and land softened, indistinguishable. Rain, unceasing.

How a flood took what was before, behind, on either side, even the woman who stood apart, looking down.

FLOOD, TRANSLATED

after *Open Passage, Closed Passage* (1977, graphite on wove paper) by Betty Goodwin

A flood can be contained by a basket, a box made of wicker, twine.

A lobster crawling into a lobster trap. The flood enters the same way.

The woman picks up the flood in the box, realizes she can't put it down.

She must carry it wherever she goes. Underworld, parking lot.

Asked what she's carrying, she'll say it's for someone else.

Someone else might look inside and see a landscape: trees, silvery calm, more trees in the distance.

A winding road, opening line of a fairy tale. Crab claw moon.

FLOOD, INTERIOR VIEW

after *Nest Two* (1973, soft-ground etching and etching on wove paper) by Betty Goodwin

Inside the flood is a knife, inside the knife is a nest, inside the nest is a story, and inside the story—

It goes on like this without end, mirror inside mirror.

When she is tired, she rests with it in her arms the way a new mother might hold a baby. Cautiously.

She remembers.

Opens it, sees the baby: blue eyelids. Rise and fall of its breathing. Ears pressed against the skull, as flowers appear under waxed paper.

A few of the men recognize the signs: if there's a swoosh, don't wait for the boom — get the hell out.

The captain and executives are elsewhere, celebrating the company's safety record: wine from Australia, shrimp on skewers.

On the rig floor, men shout as if they're lost in a forest. Sea water in the drill column, a geyser shooting into air. Four emergency calls, no answer. Around the men, no forest, just blue, blue, more blue. Cut-glass water. The *ting* of a fingernail against it.

No answer.

Swoosh of gas—

Under the surface: Mississippi Canyon 252. Where I begin speaking.

My speech has nothing to do with seven angels with seven plagues, carrying seven bowls.

Smoke is a draggled feather boa flung across sky. The exploration rig, not a production rig (damage expected to be minimal), has been heeled over for days. It sinks.

I won't tell you a story about the woman riding the many-headed creature with ten horns—you dreamed her scarlet cape, her pearls. It was a nightmare you had.

In the Gulf, the search continues for Dale, Roy, Jason, the one they called Duck. Eleven bronze hard hats will be commissioned in their memory, but not yet.

Flames on water, oil on water. Water so viscous a person could almost walk on it.

Sleep, sleep: I'll keep my voice low under your pillow.

Viva voce. Now for the turns of phrase, the sound bites. Prepare orange booms, loop them around islands and wetlands to catch what can't be caught.

What was done, what wasn't done—wrangling in the press. The downfall of Babylon, whatever. Flutes and trumpets. Are you listening?

A graceful swirl on the water, as if someone had written a name and then drawn a finger into the tail of coloured ink. Karl, Don, Shane—

I bloom
rust-brown, blood-brown. City state, kingdom, republic.

Under the water, an empire.

Try to contain my words with a hut, a roof. Lower it, fathoms down, a tower of ice crystals.

I pay no attention. I speak to the Mississippi Delta, to Breton Sound, to the Chandeleur Islands. West of the Mississippi Delta, I speak to Barataria Bay, to Isles Dernières. When the winds are from the southeast, I speak to Oyster Bayou, to Atchafalaya Bay. I speak to the sugar sand beaches, to the fringes of marram grass, to the sea oats. And the microbes in their underground realms beneath the beaches, I speak to them too. I speak to each diamond of sand, fluently, in a many-grained language.

Throughout the hearings, I'm the one who remains eloquent.

The company man answers the questions as best he can. From time to time he sips water. He doesn't hold up a picture of an oil-soaked pelican, like the Republican congressman from Louisiana.

The company man is asked what he knew, when he knew it. He answers calmly. Interminable: the hours, the tactics. Top kill, junk shots, back and forth.

At home, the congressmen mimic his accent.

Fisherman, fisherman.

Settling into him, the clotted ooze, settling into the sink, the shower, the king-sized bed in his bedroom, settling into his dreams. Into all he's given, dazzled with sea gleam, those mornings, his boat murmuring through a slit in the air between past and present.

Gravedigger's work, the work the company assigned him.
He sends the deckhands to get ice, says he'll meet them by the fuel pumps. They wait.

I speak to him on the captain's bridge, above the wheelhouse.

I speak to the Glock handgun beside him.

My speech continues, monotonously, on Live View. It doesn't show blue crabs, bottlenose dolphins, giant halibut, reddish egrets, marlin, brown pelicans, bluefin tuna, sperm whales, loggerhead turtles. But they're pulled by the undertow of my words. And above, invisible threads: I tug migrating birds, those that arrive, those that depart: piping plovers, semi-palmated sandpipers, western sandpipers, greater yellow legs, blue-winged teal, lesser yellow legs, white pelicans, lesser scaup, many ducks, many more ducks, waterwinged and marshwinged, the thousandfold panoply.

Whether I continue, or pause, or—

Stop—

Speaking altogether. Hush money to scientists for three years, a contract—

The angels of containment. Photoshopped—

Collection capacity. With a tighter sealing cap to silence—

Leaks, the possibility of seepage—

July 16, July 17, July 18. Careful monitoring—

Static kill, bullheading my words. Suing—

Relief well, as if that is the answer—

The question of dispersants—

Without compunction—

Alarms and other crucial systems not functioning at the time—

Oil is not the enemy. The enemy—

At the time, at the time—

Hush—

My voice slips in and out of your hearing, *sotto voce.* Chishui River, Great Keppel Island, Singapore Strait. And before that, Timor Sea, Norwegian Sea, Yellow Sea, any sea. Song over the waters.

Call to me.

I'll follow you.

Strike and rattle. Early ruin of crackled light. You and your brother,

a handful of stones. Sun shot through leaves, leaves, leaves,

their hundredfold ancestry. Your father and another brother,

watching. Unhurried talk, what it would take to throw a stone

halfway across the Renous, let alone hit Matchett's roof. Sun shot

through trees. Arms, quick, the toss: arc and fall. *Clang.* Waiting

for time to catch up. One drawled July day fills, seeps away. Sipped

liquor, amber-coloured glass. Your father pulls on hip waders,

one brother stands on a rock. Hand, line, hook. They cast

into crumpled foil: thirty feet, fifty. Whip and drop, whip and drop.

You've never not been by those shallows, blazing, black water farther on. A half-twist from noon to evening, sinuous winding strip

of days coming, gone, ghosted. Your dead father walking out of that

river, drenched, young. Not as he was—as he could have been.

Sky, a dance with veils: each of the veils discarded on the floor. The time of year when spirits press close.

Someone's hand, a sweeping gesture in a window.

On the street, a girl crosses a woman's shadow. *Clack, clack* of heels. The woman doesn't think herself old until the girl moves through her.

Geese skimming broken stalks in a field. Late afternoon, a kerosene lantern, smoke-smeared.

To bear responsibility, he said. I have to think about that. His voice, rowing out to sea, growing smaller.

I'd never seen him before.

Occasionally spirits fly into the mouth. They taste like frost, like honey.

A woman, a girl, a man, canted light, geese inside the canted light. I saw the man get into the rowboat. His gloved hands on the oars, ice on the water.

Soon it will cover the fields with sleep. Recurring dream, earth as cloud.

White, white, white. Our snowshoe tracks, overlapping, from barn to trees.

How simple life's become, she says. Between gloved hills, a creek. Find it

later in the woods, glossy otter. Black water over stones, under the bridge,

blood into brain. Aneurysm. Gone—the man who was living days before.

A curve in the path, single beech in a circle of spruce. Fingertips of wind,

rasp of leaves on a branch, ancient words. A kind of speech, barely heard.

Photograph

She closes the magazine, index finger marking the place.

Opens it. The monk, still burning.

Saigon, 1963. Someone had called the photographers the night before.

In the morning, two western correspondents were present.

Two monks doused Thich Quang Duc with gasoline, set him on fire.

When he died, they couldn't fit his body in a coffin. This isn't shown.

Only the monk, sitting, as flames sweep away from his face, arm, lap.

A car nearby, hood gaping. Monks and nuns at a distance.

Plastic jug of gasoline.

A man on fire, not making a sound.

Afterwards, his heart. Untouched plum.

Photographer

It seared him after the fact. Six or eight rolls of 35-millimetre film. A sequence, from the beginning—shock in the monk's eyes as his face caught fire—through to the blackened corpse at the end. How he was prepared and not prepared. How the monk remained still throughout. Stink of gas and burning flesh. People wailing, prostrating themselves. Later, at sunset, a vision of Buddha seated in the sky. If not for the photographer, John F. Kennedy wouldn't have had the picture on his desk the following day, wouldn't have spoken to the U.S. ambassador to Vietnam, about to leave for Saigon. Trying to stop what had already begun. The years of what followed, and the photographer's belief he'd had a hand in it, in someone's death, as if he'd picked up the plastic jug that morning and poured a clear stream of gasoline over another man's head.

Photograph

Palm trees, humid air.

Nowhere near the furnace room, where a girl sits with stacks of magazines.
Flipping through February 11, 1966 (here's a slim woman, with matching apron and
oven mitts, taking a pie from the oven), opens to

Private First Class, Thomas Cole, a medic, who tilts a tin cup of water to the mouth
of Staff Sergeant Harrison Pell. Lying in the dirt near An Thai, Binh Dinh
Province. Operation Masher.

The medic can't see because of the bandage, but he holds the cup for the other,
whose head rests on his thigh. Boys—

about nine or ten years older than the girl—

bound together. Ouroboros.

Photographer

The man who tells the story (see how the paratrooper's body in one of his photographs hangs on its cable, pulled up to the helicopter, turning drowsily as it goes) is the story itself. Part Vietnamese, part French. Split man, hanged man. Always his half-smile, withheld. His photograph of a body in air, slow-moving clock. And the one not taken, showing what hasn't happened yet (near Khe Sanh over the Ho Chi Minh Trail, when a helicopter dropped into trees after being shot down by the Viet Cong). A photographer's body, never found, except for bits of bone that might have been those of other photographers. Teeth in the dirt, as if the past had devoured the future.

Photograph

Air. Piled up, downy.

And below, a sheen over rectangles of rice paddies.

But it's the clouds. Temples, each with its Buddha. Carved elephants, dragons, and chrysanthemums. Courtyards. Light.

This is the photograph she took from the helicopter, over the Mekong Delta.

Not Wisconsin, but something that reminded her. Fields, afternoon,

long haul of hours. Out of the clouds, a throng.

Swarm of helicopters moving through the temples, through the elephants, dragons, and chrysanthemums.

Photographer

With pearls in her ears, a woman (photographer, pilot, one of the boys) lies on the ground near Chu Lai. Carotid artery torn open, blood seeping under her arm, her face. Invisible: her friend, who takes the photograph as she dies. The chaplain for the U.S. Marine Corps bends his head, a woman splayed at his feet, three marines watching: two standing, one sitting. Strict perfection of the composition. The chaplain's hand—the vanishing point—about to make the sign of the cross, but not yet.

Some days he is quite lucid. He thinks about thinking.

What it is to be.

What it is to have some of the thinking erased.

Thinking aslant, knowing he used to be able to think differently.

Cities of thoughts vanish. Each day, whole cities.

He thinks about how we try to stand apart from our thinking.

Sometimes we look down on our thinking from above. Being objective.

Dividing the rational from the irrational.

He tests himself, thinking.

He imagines God thinking.

It's not God he wants to think about.

He thinks about the bacon hissing and curling in the frying pan.

The worst thing he can imagine is not being able to think clearly.

Not thinking clearly is one of the worst forms of pain.

He has yet to enter the city of pain, but he can see its towers and domes.

And beyond, the city of oblivion.

He gazes at the ducks on the tabletop of the estuary instead.

Wishes he could get through.

Forgets,   Early, a little mist burning off

    , what (

).

                            A button. Doesn't know.

                            ~~White~~

~~button, silver rim. How.~~

Do up a small fish, magic

lamp?

                            Glass, antique, his mother's. Touched with.

                            He can't do up his button. Runs his finger

                            over his mother's

                            fruit bowl, glass, antique

someone, himself   ,   ,   moving in a mirror.

Walks outside, cloudy, jade-coloured.

He finds her crying in the bedroom with the lights out. He puts his arms around her. No sound, except all they can't say. The neighbour's house turns into a ship, listing. Starboard, port, starboard. O of moon, forked shadows imitating trees. He doesn't speak about how the rug is being pulled out from under him. Nothing beneath the rug, nothing to stop him falling through space. A dream, no end to it.

A woman, wakened by nurses
—rubber-soled shoes on tile—

surfaces in an ocean, pain folding and unfolding in the centre of her body.

Wakened by mortals.

Flared skirt of light on a street by the hospital. A taxi, nowhere to go.
Wasting time.

As if the city were at the end of the ocean. Rising, falling.

Wasting away. Rocked on water, a woman,
arms circling her ribs. The soul's wing-case, dark
glass of each moment.

Who will take her place, in this unmoored boatbed, in the small
of the small hours?

Across the continent, a prairie lane unrolls to water's edge, ice-plated. Hay bales in the field, stippled white: fixed earth, dead-weight.

Too early, winter.

When snow geese rise, obscuring the sandhill cranes, air is shaken pepper and salt.

Sky, released.

An answer to the question posed by ground.

The nurse turns the woman to one side, bathes her,
turns her to the other side.

The boat dips, bobs.

Quiet patter. A voice reserved for those lying down.

Flatland, taut with cold, crops not yet taken in. Whooping cranes, scroll of black-tipped wings against snow.

Leaving this place, leaving.

One cry, hundreds: elsewhere, elsewhere.

Slate-grey clouds, windlessness. Nothing to write with, even if she wanted to. Flowers, cards. Nothing she needs.

Visitors come to the door, leave, come to the door again.

She wakes, snow on her bed.

Snow geese lift over Muskiki, about to fly the length of the Great Plains.

Many wings. Carrying the future to the past,
time locked by time, the bolt shot across plumed cloud. It echoes.

She brushes snow from her face. Wet skin.

What to say to the children?

No one walks the frost-sparkled road by the hospital. A dog barks
to be let inside.

No refuge.

She sleeps a drugged sleep. Her sister's hand nested,
held.

The nurses speak with their hands, gently.

She journeys. Goes in and out of her body,
through a different door each time. Hears
water, its lapping clocks. Hears boats thumping against boats. The lighting
of paper lanterns.

Constellations, opening and closing.

Sand flats, river. Twilight, crushed saffron. Last hour of the day, the last

sandhill cranes draw sky after them as they arrive.
Burbling cry upon cry, layers of cries. Wheel and settle, wheel and settle.

The same questions asked

before the spirit's journey
into the afterlife. Did you bring joy?

Did you find joy?

Yes.

Hold her. Pick her up in your arms.

Yes.

Already
she casts the far light of stars.

Carry her, carry her.

Sandhill cranes sweep over low hills, smoke-coloured. Cirrus
feathers. Dawn

or dusk? Wings pulling air, puckering air.

They descend, descend, descend.

Lay sky's silver on water's silver, one slipped into the other.

She tells me of a dream. A man carrying tea on a tray, and the host,
derisive.

How she got up from her chair, angry. Walked a road along the sea. Dolphins
over water, under, over: bracelets of bodies. And above, birds—

How did they take shape out of a white sky?
Paper, creased sharply.

How did they know when to migrate, when to move on?

Later, an answering dream.

I unlocked a cabinet, opened my ribs.
From a many-branching tree: finches, warblers, kingfishers. One pelican.

They flew off. I distracted myself by setting a table, taking goblets
and dishes from the cabinet: no end to what I could take.

And the tree that held the birds?

This was a dream, remember.

In a dream, the day after this one passes through
the day before.

This is how we wake.

Chocolate eggs in red foil on the table, others hidden in the living room.

A robin pecks, pecks; a birdhouse hangs, tilted, on the elm closest to the house. A man makes pancakes, sausages, puts them on a plate. Now he bends to brush and brush and brush a white cat. A winding curve between the man's legs: the cat, released. A curve in Ella Fitzgerald's voice.

One, two, three curves made by an oxbow river, meandering through the coulee we saw the day before, a day furred with animal haunches of the slopes, sage greening under dead stalks. In evening, tired after hiking, we sat at the kitchen table. Grey moths tap-tapping messages on the screen.

The table, the lamp, a full glass in my hand: dark crimson, sweetsour.
Moths in hooded capes.
Joy, sorrow.

Now, on the steps, the white cat watches the robin. My friend laughs, offers raspberries. Swoops up, the robin, and two boys tumble out of a tree beyond the back lane, run away. Their bodies are jokes and pranks. Ella sings.

Sorrow in the dry grass, joy between the trees.

Once, before waking, I saw the tree. Its branches could have been made by a jeweller.
Wild dark, coyote dark, and a tree, glowing. Northern lights, ice-thin

music. No woodcutter in this story. Only the tree, taller than any other,

inside you.

Not the one outside the kitchen window, skirts high above the ground.
The tamarack's dropped needles, pulling gold threads under snow.

Not the Wonderboom, ancient fig, surrounded by its ring of daughters. Not the
Dragon Tree of Icod de los Vinos. Not the Arbre de Ténéré, last acacia of the desert.

Inside the night cathedral of your life

is a tree without name—carrying the names of other trees—a tree candled, on fire,
but not burning.

Brushed with radiance,
each branch, each tassel, the tip of each needle.

I

My mother and I held hands, looking at him. Hair, not combed the way he'd

have combed it. They'd put something between his lips to keep them closed.

A kind of glue. The pink sheet, neatly folded across his chest, was meant

to cover the makeshift coffin so we wouldn't see it. Soon they'd send his body

to the crematorium. Once or twice I'd seen him asleep in his chair on the porch,

a newspaper on his lap. If a squirrel chattered in the ravine, he'd waken, snap open

the business section. This wasn't sleep. Neither of us cried; we were still. Alone,

together. Her fingers moved against my hand, secret animals trying to find a home.

II

Before the funeral service began, my sister talked to the minister, a close

friend. She leaned forward on the edge of her folding chair, lush fragrance

of white roses veiling the room. It could have been a hotel lobby. Where

had death taken him? I saw him walking a beach in Maine, but he didn't

inhabit that photograph, taken years before. The minister looked at my sister

kindly, tilting his head, a sheen on his hair. During the service, he played

the Mass in B Minor—the best music ever written, so my father said. Bach

was blind when he finished it; he was near death. Later I stood with my aunt

by the coffin. Crumbs handed back and forth as words. I could have said,

Kyrie, Gloria. I could have said, *Hosanna, Benedictus, Agnus Dei.*

III

Two weeks after he died, I went to stay in the mountains. On a path, people

appeared and vanished. A dark-haired girl put her hand to her mouth

as she laughed. Afterwards, a scent of cedar. Low sounds in the night, as if

the blue-grey mountains were wolfish dogs, sleeping. Now and then, one

would thump a hind leg, rhythmically, on a hard floor. I was outside a dream;

I was dreamt. Sometimes I wanted a cigarette, just to watch the smoke.

Magpies: black, white, black. I studied photographs in a book, learning

to dwell in the world of trees. Clear, clean mornings. For a time, I lived

inside a leaf on the crown of a lithe aspen. The leaf was silk-thin, twirling.

—with the ending poised inside the beginning.

First aria. In July, a leaf falling but not falling, one

finger's length of scarlet about to skim the pond's

ink. Foreshadowing, he thinks. An opening

into dense plots and subplots

of green. *My dear*

one—

Is it

a story at all

or a glimpse there

from the window of a train? (In

her notebook, an aria written in Anna

Magdalena's hand.) Out of the woods: whale

backs of slabbed mud, Tantramar's tasselled grasses,

two kestrels stitching air. Sarabande. Here, the leaf's

languid spin. Lavish, improbable. Moment before

the moment after: a dropped leaf on water.

This is what we're made of:

unlit dust of stars.

Blood,

bone.

Salt

on skin. Taste

honeysuckle by the shed.

Swinging door, red-handled spade,

up-ended lawn chair tethered by stitchwort

(a nebula), winding strands of vetch. *Please don't*

worry about me——An electrical storm approaching from

the west. Self turned inside out. Cumulonimbus sheets on

the clothesline, a woman plucking pegs. Shades her eyes. Why

so much light when it's about to rain? Single hummingbird

at the feeder, ruby-throated, no bigger than a child's hand:

small, smaller, smallest. *Canone all'Unisuono.*

Coherence, or the illusion of coherence

that comes before

chaos.

The man

sees this the way

God might see if God could

see lightning as a story without prologue,

climax, dénouement. O, bright string. Shivered air.

The ordinary settles into corners, a sleeping cat. Nearly

hidden pleasures of each life. Open-faced dahlias in a vase

(Waterford), sour mash whisky at the bottom of a glass,

a ring. Contrapuntal self. She's playing the same

thing over and over. Difficult to slow it

down. Her heart. Her father's

Steinway

in

need of tuning.

Can't sleep, recalling that

anguished letter about the Spanish Civil

War. One priest killed after capture; the other shot

after they'd freed him, after they told him to get lost.

She imagines his jerky gait, mud-crusted boots, bloody

spatters on his soutane: raven-man descending the rock-

strewn slope, left, right, breath of wind, nape—

Moment before the moment after.

The dead tell

tales

in the bodies

of the living. The man steps

off the train, waves to his brother, who

leans against his pickup. Glints of chrome, tarred

islands on pavement. Goldenrod in ditches. *I don't*

much like tests—Faint rush of nausea. Could be the heat.

A glassy shape floats before him, turning, almost transparent.

His own cells, never to be folded into someone else's.

Her waterfall hands on the keys, cascading.

Canone alla Seconda. But

nothing

much changes. Her cat

wants out, cries to come back in. Tulle

crinolines in the sky, rain about to——Why trust

anyone who makes her so angry? She speaks fiercely to

the mirror, erases a galaxy of spots with a towel. Slams

the famous playwright's biography (his owlish face) on

the tiled floor. Tears in her eyes. Once, he called her

that self inside his own self, but larger.

Exploding the self he thought

he was.

His brother

smokes rolled cigarettes.

Steers the truck with one knee, runs his

tongue along the paper's edge. Uncanny likeness,

brother to brother. One of them off the hook, the other

with a riddle in the genes, hole in a pocket of their father's

navy jacket, hanging in the closet. Lost in the lining:

darkened pennies, string, tickets, a folded and

refolded letter. Onion skin. Traces.

My love—A woman's

body

making up a

story with or without her

consent. Yowling cat. Fingertips of rain,

glass. Wet patterns printed on the steps, hundreds

of thousands. What it means. No whistling up a child.

He doesn't want damage. She turns off the kettle—*not*

necessarily conclusive. Room for interpretation—Hers, his.

The cat, inside, winds and winds through her legs.

He's gone. Two loops, a figure eight.

Wet fur against her skin.

She wants

to

be held

in someone's arms,

swung around, swung around,

held in someone's arms. Father, brother,

sister, mother. Wants to hold a lover, a baby. Selves,

one inside another. Held within. Holding. And swung

around—He wants her, but knows what's growing deep

in his body. Three crows. Dust on the road, dervishes

ghosting behind the truck, sparkles of grit. Now

they stop at his brother's place. Hollyhocks,

rose-pink ears. Bees drift in

and out of

hives

at the field's

edge. He gets out, dazed,

recalls her at the inlaid Italian desk

after the funeral. Musk of lilies. His mother,

head bent over her task, pen making its way across

each piece of thick notepaper, rowboat over ocean.

And the clock, the clock, the clock. *Thank you*

for your kind—The bees are lifting air,

lifting it into last light. First

light. A woman

sweeps

a goldfinch into

the dustpan. The cat again.

She thinks of the priest walking out

of his life, hearing the shot and not hearing it.

Furiously, she digs a hole the size of her hand. What

balance is possible in opposition? *Canone alla Quarto.*

(High voice leads, low voice follows; they change later.)

What does her life have to do with the life of a writer,

hauled off early one morning? Granada,

1936. The writer, a teacher,

and

two *banderilleros,*

absent from the photograph.

Gone, too, the men who came for them.

The wagon, horses. She's studied that puzzle

of olive trees, shadows fallen to pieces on silver-

white ground where the writer, teacher, *banderilleros*

might be buried. Invisible skulls, a scattering

of holes, where bullets came and went.

What does one

life

have to do—

Here are the man's sleepy

nephews at the table, one with his head laid

beside a bowl, blue eye unblinking. The spoon

clinks against china. The man plays the part of uncle,

a coin hidden in his left ear, taken out of his right. Spun,

tossed, clapped on his hand. Do it again, the boys

plead. Do it! He opens his palm. Vanished.

But where? She tucks the sun-

bright, feathered

body

into earth, cells

disintegrating. DNA—broken

ladder. Her grandmother's framed picture

of saints climbing, rung by rung, into a new role

as clouds, guardian angels of clouds. Spidery demons

try to shake them loose before they get there. Goodness

accompanied by its twin. Who cares about the tiny afterlife

of a finch (complex, frenetic, music) now that crumbled

soil covers its body? Spattering of bugs, greenish-yellow

glue marking the truck's windshield. Late morning.

He broods, unlike his brother. Canon

in contrary motion.

River

rider, a heron spreads

twelfth-century wings. The man

can't open a door in the day, go home. Takes

cold beer out of the cooler, some sandwiches, unwraps

the homemade cookies. Their lives might be nothing more

than a history of cells. Dividing, multiplying. Unless. *Canone alla Quinta.* Endings, a melancholy. Muddied boots, a man

walking, one step closer to gun-crack, echoes. As if

one person's life could be someone else's.

A bird's body in her palm. Candle,

flare. *My love*—Folded

and re-

folded letter.

She's inside, outside the self

he is now. Breaking him. His parents'

stories, written in his cells, aren't the only ones.

Blood, bone, salt, skin. Dust. He finds a ham sandwich,

eats it, gazes north. Hair, loosened, on a pillow. River. In

time, out of time. *Canone alla Settima.* He wants to be held

in someone's arms. His chest opens, the river's current

slides through. He lets it. Finishes the sandwich.

River netted into delta. Slip, slipping,

slipped into ocean. He's ocean.

lets himself be held.

Held

by what she knows,

one blazing leaf—falling, not

falling—she lets him go. Knows that he

arrives, departs, within her. Married, unmarried.

Variatio 25, rare black pearl. She gets up, wipes a hand

on her jeans. Catches the screen door behind her so it won't

slam. He'll call; he knows the test results. Nothing as it was.

Clear. A slow line of notes: she remembers how it goes.

Tonight, a cat's bowl of moon. Blue. She lets dirty

fingers drift over the piano's keys. Spool

of last notes. *Aria da capo.*

A beginning

poised

inside the ending

poised inside the beginning—

For the sequence of poems called *"Life* Magazine" I am indebted to the work of several photographers who faced extremely challenging conditions during the Vietnam War: American photographer Malcolm Browne; French-Vietnamese photographer Henri Huet; and the first female American war photographer to be killed in action, Dickey Chapelle. One book was particularly helpful in my research: *Requiem: By the Photographers Who Died in Vietnam and Indochina,* edited by Horst Faas and Tim Page.

In the fall of 2009, it was my privilege to see whooping cranes among flocks of sandhill cranes and snow geese near Saskatoon, Saskatchewan—birds that figure prominently in "Boat of Dawn, Boat of Dusk." I am indebted to Dianne Miller and to the Nature Society of Saskatoon for that field trip.

For the same poem, I learned that during the period of the New Kingdom, Egyptians believed that a series of questions were asked in the Hall of Truth, where souls came before Osiris to be judged in a ritual known as the Weighing of the Heart. I am grateful to Liz Klinck for bringing two of those questions to my attention.

For "Double Helix," I owe a debt to Glenn Gould's interpretation of Bach's *Goldberg Variations,* which informed and helped structure the entire poem. I am also indebted to Simone Weil's letters about the Spanish Civil War. In the same poem, Frederico García Lorca is referred to as the writer taken from his home in Granada. (Lorca disappeared on August 19, 1936, and is presumed to have been executed that day.)

ACKNOWLEDGEMENTS

I was allowed the time to write these poems because of generous support from the Canada Council and from the Nova Scotia Department of Tourism, Culture and Heritage.

"Book of Beginnings" was shown together with the abstract photographs of John Berridge in an exhibit at the Lyghtesome Gallery, in Antigonish, Nova Scotia, in October 2008. Thanks to Beth and Jeff Parker for making this exhibit possible.

Some of these poems were first published in the following literary reviews: *Arc, CV2, Prairie Fire, Prism international, The Fiddlehead, The Literary Review of Canada,* and *The Malahat Review.*

As always, thanks to Don McKay for his attentive listening and gracious comments, and for the way he nudges a book closer to what it wants to be.

I am also grateful to friends and writers who have helped with certain poems: Linda Clarke, Lorri Neilsen Glenn, Aislinn Hunter, and Kate Waters. Special thanks to Karin Cope, for her gift of a phtograph.

For the loving support of my mother, Janet, my sisters and their families, and, especially, for Paul, David, and Sarah—my deepest thanks.

——

"The Hives" is for Barry Brown.

"Tonja's Letter" is for Tonja Gunvaldsen Klaassen.

"Easter" is for Anne McDonald and Dave Sealy.

"In the Night Cathedral, a Tree" is for Roberta Wells.

"Boat of Dawn, Boat of Dusk" is in memory of Annette Ahern.

"Clear" is in memory of my father, John R. Simpson.